ACKNOWLEDGEMENTS

I am very grateful to John Fitzgerald, Cecily Blench, and Age Concern Leominster for technical assistance at various stages, and also to Jean Hardy, Stuart Masters, Geoffrey Morries, and very especially to Ken, for suggestions about the text, also at different stages. Any errors and omissions are, of-course, my own responsibility.

Many thanks are due to Ian Jackson, Librarian of Woodbrooke Quaker Study Centre for patience in finding resources in the Quaker Library.

Some of this material has been published previously in the Friends Quarterly, issues October 1998 and August 2011, for which I am also grateful.

IS THERE NOT A NEW CREATION ?

The Experience of Early Friends

Anne Adams

i

Published by

Applegarth Publications
The Folley
Luston
Herefordshire
HR6 0BX

2012

ISBN 978-0-9570408-0-9

Cover design by Ken Adams

Orphans Press
Leominster, Herefordshire
HR6 0LD

FSC paper

CONTENTS

1. INTRODUCTION

The first period of Quakerism is, to me, the most exciting and interesting. Much has been written about it, from various points of view, some of which will be outlined here. Just as George Fox wrote that one cannot understand the writings of the Bible unless one is in the spirit in which they were written, so it is difficult for us to understand early Friends beliefs, as the spirit of our materialistic age is so far removed from theirs. To them everything seemed new and exciting, discoveries in science had not dimmed the imagination, religious beliefs were of vital importance, and many theories abounded about God and the universe.

Where early Friends got their beliefs from, how this vision became lost, and especially what happened to the feeling of unity with the creation (see Note 1) which was experienced by early Friends are fascinating subjects for investigation.

Rufus M. Jones in several writings, but especially in *Spiritual Reformers in the 16th & 17th Centuries* (p. 336) traces early Friends beliefs to a tradition of mysticism following the continental mystics and spiritualists, whereas others (Tolles 1961 p. xxvii) believe that Quakerism was a natural outgrowth from Puritanism.

Another view put forward by Douglas Gwyn (1984 p. xiii- xxiii), who summarises the other two theories in some detail, is that early Friends, particularly Fox, took up the belief that "Christ has come to teach his people himself". They acted on it, and that the kingdom of God is here now, spreading their prophetic message throughout the country.

A more specific source for the beliefs of early Friends can be found in the myth of the "everlasting gospel" and the three stages of history. This incorporates the immediacy of Gywn's views, but reaches to their source. This myth, which dates to Joachim of Fiori going back at least to the twelfth century (Hill p. 147), gives a coherent and all-inclusive basis for the inspiration of early Friends. It was a holistic belief in that it covered the history of the relationships between God and humans and included the whole of creation, as exemplified by paradise. The origin of Fox's concept of "gospel order" can also be linked to the everlasting gospel.

The idea of a covenant between God and humans was important. There are many points in the Bible where covenants with God are described, but early Friends believed in a new covenant for the New Creation, which replaced the old covenants, and portrayed a loving and forgiving God.

1

Early Friends seem to have undergone a paradigm shift of attitude which carried over into their behaviour so that they were actually living in the New Creation, regardless of the contradictions surrounding them.

I feel that it is extremely sad that this holistic vision was almost entirely lost, and is not generally referred to by later writers on Quakerism. It seems to have been due to a number of factors: the onset of "The Age of Reason", which affected Quakers as well as others, and fear of being confused with the Ranters, are two. The publication in 1676 of Barclay's *Apology* (Robert Barclay 1648-1690) was also influential, as it appears to have tried to reassure its readers that Friends were not an outlandish fanatical sect, but were quite respectable worthy members of society. The New Creation would not have fitted in with this image.

From the 18th century until recently, very little occurs in writings by Quakers about relationships with the whole of creation. The vision of the New Creation was lost, together with references to nature and God's relationship to it. Writers have concentrated on the relationship between God and humans almost exclusively. However, more recently a number of writers (Gwyn, Keiser, Schurman, Wilson, Morries in particular), have rediscovered the inclusiveness of early Friends vision.

This booklet will show that early Friends had a holistic view of creation, and that the natural world took a more prominent place in their vision than has been recognised previously. The holistic belief of early Friends is particularly relevant today when we see so much destruction of the rest of creation due to human arrogance, ignorance and selfishness. The value of the rest of creation is being realised now, but anthropocentrically, rather than with a true appreciation of the beauty and the intricate relationships within the whole of nature.

The book is divided into 9 chapters. The second describes the context in which early Friends lived their lives. Chapters 3 and 4 describe the basis of early Friends' beliefs, tracing them to writings in 12th- 13th century Italy, Chapter 3 concentrating on the New Creation and Chapter 4 on the Everlasting Gospel. Chapters 5, 6 and 7 describe the results of the vision of the "New Creation" and how it affected other aspects of the lives of early Friends. One is on animals, one on education, and one on praise poems. The eighth chapter is on the fading of the vision. The last chapter discusses early Friends' experience and its relevance for us today.

2. CONTEXT

To get an indication of the historical context in which early Friends emerged one has to look at the situation which existed in the 17th Century. This is well described by Christopher Hill (1975) as "the world turned upside down". It was a time of turmoil and questioning of the established church, particularly between 1640 and 1660. There was relative freedom of speech and thought, and many small sects and groups developed, often around one individual. Religion was taken very seriously and people were anxiously searching for the truth, arguing and disputing, forming new groups, or joining old ones. Hill states that a Quaker of the early 1650s had more in common with a Leveller, a Digger or a Ranter than with a modern member of the Society of Friends (p. 14). New ideas had come in from the continent of Europe, translated into English, so there was an awareness of alternatives to the Puritan church which was then dominant. Many were disillusioned with this church and the frequent ignorance and lack of vision of many of the ministers. Millenarianism was a common belief with hopes for a new more just and equal society. Into this milieu came George Fox and others searching for a truth to live by.

There are several schools of thought concerning the influences on early Friends. One was held by Rufus Jones, that they were affected by the "spiritual reformers" of the 16th and 17th centuries. Another is that their beliefs are a natural outgrowth from Protestantism. This is shown in a comparison with two editions of Braithwaite's *The Second Period of Quakerism*. In the first edition (1921) Rufus Jones emphasises the mystical and prophetic aspects of Quakerism. (Jones p. xxiv et seq.). He writes that early Friends took the unorganised stage of apostolic Christianity as their model, contrasting it with the creeds, hierarchy, external sacraments and corruptions of the medieval church. Their church was built on those who experienced the Holy Spirit and on the expanding revelation of God through men. He elaborates this belief in *Spiritual Reformers*, quoting many of those who wrote in favour of a "spiritual" type of religion and against the rigidity of the Protestant church, which had, he believed, become as dependent on ritual and external forms as the Catholic church against which it had rebelled.

Jones quotes a number of these "spiritual reformers" and especially concentrates on Jacob Boehme (p.151-234), whose vision was very similar to Fox's, and some of whose phrases seem to be echoed by Fox. Jones relates that Boehme went to a public green near his house "and there it seemed to him that he could see into the very heart and secret of Nature, and that he could behold the innermost properties of things" (p. 159).

Of later experiences Boehme writes:-

> In one quarter of an hour I saw and knew more
> than if I had been many years together in a
> University. . . I saw and knew the Being of Beings,
> the Byss and Abyss, the eternal generation of the
> Trinity, the origin and descent of the world, and of
> all creatures through Divine Wisdom.
> (p. 159).

Both Boehme's and Fox's vision are concerned with sudden insight into the natural world and its value, and the uses of various plants. Fox seems to have felt that he entered into the paradise from which Adam and Eve were banished. Both received an intuitive knowledge outside the realm of reason. Rufus Jones compares Fox and Boehme in some depth, and concludes that their ideas and experiences were very similar (p. 221 et seq.).

In the 1961 and subsequent editions of *The Second Period*, the tide has turned against Rufus Jones, whose ideas are thrown out in favour of an indigenous Puritan outgrowth. Though recognising Jones' wide scholarship, Tolles states that recent studies point to Quakerism as being a natural development from Puritanism. He writes that modern research has turned away from the "problematical, continental and mystical roots of Quakerism and come to focus on its more immediate English Puritan origins" (Braithwaite 1961, p. xxvi). Tolles states that "Quakerism was a natural, almost predictable outgrowth of Puritanism". This thesis is also held by others, including Hugh Barbour and Geoffrey Nuttall (Braithwaite, p. xxvii).

It does not appear that those who supported the Protestant origins saw any connection with the natural world, but Jones certainly has an inkling of this in his quotes from Fox and Boehme. However, he puts these in his category of mystical experiences rather than a connection with the whole of creation. In a later work (1932 p.16) Jones states that in the period of the English Commonwealth, 1640-1660 (also the flowering time of early Friends), there were four main driving forces in what he calls "A Great Awakening". These were: a revival of faith, humanism, the Puritan movement, and a "pantheistical sentiment" which was evident both on the Continent and in England (see Note 2) so here he does see a connection with nature.

Gwyn, like Jones, disagrees with the Protestant basis. He points out that Barclay, in his *Apology* and his attempt to make some doctrinal coherence from the enthusiastic writings of early Friends, put Quaker theology into a Puritan framework and in so doing he lost the apocalyptic fervour of their witness. As Gwyn writes "the operation was a success, but the patient died, or at least was not the same person any longer" (1998, p. 135).

Gwyn points to a third possibility, that early Friends, Fox in particular, based their beliefs on the phrase from Fox that "Christ has come to teach his people himself". (1991, p. xxii). As Gwyn acknowledges, the originator of this suggestion was Lewis Benson (Benson 1976, p. 3). From this came the vision of the early Quaker movement as a prophetic community, much like that enjoyed by the first disciples. (Gwyn 1991, p. xxiii).

A particular view about the beliefs of early Friends on their relationships with the rest of creation is put forward by Geoffrey Nuttall (1947). He discusses the section in the Journal when John Story offered Fox a pipe of tobacco, which he accepted lest Storey should say that Fox "had not unity with the creation" (Nickalls p.110). Nuttall says that the conception of a divine harmony in creation was fashionable at the time.

This shaded off into Rosicrucianism, magic and quackery at one end, but at the other developed into the study of various sciences. Nuttall also says that Fox had knowledge of the book on Hermetic Medecine published in 1655 by Henry Vaughan, the poet, as a translation of the book by Heinrich Nolle. The title Hermetic was taken from the Eqyptian God, Hermes Trismegistus. This stated that everything in nature has its place in the divine ordering, that beasts and birds, trees and herbs, even stones:

> are all held together in
> That busie Commerce kept between
> God and his creatures, though unseen.

From Vaughan's poem "The Stone" (Nuttall p.136). See also the note in Braithwaite in *The Beginnings...* (p. 553).

Vaughan (1621-1695) was a contemporary of Fox, and Nuttall compares their ideas. The Hermetic writers did not believe that the rest of creation had been involved in Adam's fall, but they also did not believe that humans had been restored by the new creation, so they envied nature for its innocence. (Nuttall p. 138).

Edward Bourne, a friend of Fox's, wrote in 1656, that Fox spoke of Eqyptian learning and had a deep and wonderful understanding of natural and spiritual things. (Nuttall p. 139).

Some kind of influence by the Hermeticists seems quite credible as it would fit in with early Friends beliefs about the creation and the place of humans in it. In other matters, however, Friends differed from the Hermeticists.

With regard to the poets of the time, Jones in *Spiritual Reformers...*(p. 320 et seq.) has a chapter on poets including Traherne, Herbert, Vaughan, Crashaw, and Quarles in which he compares their poetry with the writings of others in his book. They also felt a unity with the whole of creation, and that "Eternity" is here with us now. This description sounds very similar to the "New Creation", though these particular words are not stated.

To return to the beginnings of Quakerism, there is another view of its continental origins. This starts with the dedication of a monk, Joachim, working in the 13th century in Fiori, Calabria. For details see the next chapter.

3. THE THREE STAGES OF HISTORY AND THE NEW CREATION

The myth of the new creation and the everlasting gospel point to a specific origin for Quaker beliefs. Both these concepts come from *Revelation*, (21.1 the new creation, 14.6, the everlasting gospel) but were given actuality as far back as the 13th Century in Calabria and persisted throughout four centuries, to re-emerge in another language in 17th century England, as will be described below.

The following account is drawn mostly from *Studies in Mystical Religion* by Rufus Jones (p.171-6) with additions from Heer, who also gives a description of the concept of the Eternal Gospel and the New Creation. The idea originated with Joachim of Floris (Fiori) in Calabria, originally a Cistercian. He became dissatisfied with the worldliness of the order at the time and founded a stricter one emphasising poverty and simplicity. After careful study of the Bible he had a vision which involved three stages of history, two past and the third to come. The first age was that of the Church of the Father, beginning with Adam and ending with Zacharias. This was the age of slaves, fear, starlight, winter and nettles ! The second, the Church of the Son, was the age of sons, faith, dawn, spring and roses. The third stage was the age of the Holy Ghost and was just about to dawn. This was the age of friends, love, full day, glorious summer and lilies. This third stage would be a time of peace and truth over the whole earth.

Joachim calculated that there would be a sudden spiritual expansion in 1260, in which a new order of men would arise, knowing the will of the spirit. (The date 1260 was calculated as being 42 generations of 30 years each between Adam and Christ). They would not require mediators or even the scriptures as they would see "face to face" and have unbroken communion with God. He called it the "Spiritual Gospel of Christ, the Gospel of the Kingdom, and sometimes "The Eternal Gospel" (Jones, *Studies*…) This new age would also be one of unity between God, humans and the creation.

Joachim died in 1202, but left behind a little group of disciples who produced more books, which were taken away in 1240 to a Franciscan monastery in Pisa for safe keeping. A small group within the Franciscan circle, known as the "Spirituals", made links with the Joachimites and carried the idea of the three stages forward, and giving a vivid picture of the glory of the new age, which was just breaking. The new order would be heralded by the preaching of the "eternal gospel". The system was written down by Gerard of San Donnino, a friar from Pisa who was studying in Paris, and in 1254 the book, the "Eternal Gospel" was published. This consisted partly of his own writings and partly of Joachim's. It stated that the new age would supersede all previous ages, the whole church system would be swept away, and the religion of the Spirit would take its place. The Spiritual Franciscans would become the successors of the papal church (Heer p. 231).

It is interesting that Jones mentions the "Spirituals" in *Spiritual Reformers…* (p. 31) calling them "sixteenth century Quakers", but does not connect them with Joachim. He regards the millennial hopes and expectations as "misguided" and states that the Spirituals laboured to check them, which may account for his failure to see a connection with the seventeenth century Quakers. This seems very interesting and further research is needed on the connections between the "Spirituals" and the

Joachimites, as according to Heer, the Spirituals took up the vision of the new creation and made it their own. Heer gives quite a long description of their history and struggles against persecution (pp. 287-291).

Rather to be expected, the book "The Eternal Gospel" was condemned as heretical by the established church, and ordered to be burned and Gerard was condemned to life imprisonment in 1255 (Heer p. 231). The Spirituals were generally persecuted, and fled to Spain, Southern France and Italy, sometimes linking with other radical sects.

Following their persecution the Franciscan Spirituals underwent a period of intellectual and spiritual unrest and of speculation which fostered the scientific studies of Roger Bacon and the philosophical and political theorising of William of Ockam (Heer p. 231).

> The study of natural science was one means of "remaking the world" in the Spiritual Franciscan sense. In Roger Bacon and his pupil, Arnold of Villanova the prophetic enthusiam of the Spirituals was diverted to the aquisition of knowledge which could alone enable its possessors to remake the world. The only true learning was that of the man learned in nature; it was he who truly understood the spirit, since he uncovered it where it lay at the heart of nature; he would usher in the New Age, the Age of Man, whose spirit would conquer the earth. (Heer p. 291).

This led later to the development of an exploitative attitude, somewhat different from Joachim's gentler spiritual vision.

Joachim's vision persisted for many centuries. He is placed by Dante in Paradise (see Note 3) and Columbus took him as a patron for his Indian undertaking (Heer p. 156). He was obviously an original thinker and initiator of ideas and is referred to by Heer as "one of the first great philosophers of history" (p. 61).

The millenarian hopes of the 17th Century which derived from Joachim are described in detail by Hill (1975). He states that "By the middle of the century a consensus seems to have been reached, indicating the advent of remarkable events in the mid 1650s: the fall of Antichrist, perhaps the second coming and the millennium" (p. 92). He also quotes Nuttall and others who believed that "the spread of Quakerism in the 1650s would have been impossible without the antecedent millenarian excitement" (p. 97). So the 17th Century was fertile ground for the seed of the coming of the New Creation and the Everlasting Gospel, which Hill describes. The New Creation, or the third age was the present one, "in which the Holy Spirit was coming into the hearts of all men to free them from existing forms and ordinances" (p. 147). Hill quotes Winstanley, whose ideas were probably typical of the times.

Virginia Schurman (1990) sees how early Friends beliefs included the three stages of history and the connection with the whole of creation, but she does not mention the eternal gospel. She writes in detail about three stages. In the first stage God was the teacher to Adam and Eve in the Garden of Eden. Adam and Eve were particularly important in maintaining the original harmony, goodness and blessedness of the creation. They were given animals and plants to provide them with food, and were to be guided by divine wisdom as to their use.

In the Fall Satan became the second teacher, as Adam and Eve sought to live by their own wisdom, rather than God's. They let wickedness and unrighteousness destroy the goodness and order of the creation. So people abused the creatures and ruled over them, not in the wisdom of God, as Burrough writes (Schurman p. 33).

The third teacher was Christ, who gives the power to overcome Satan (Schurman p. 33). Fox had experienced this victory, and realised that only this Inward Teacher, the Light would lead him out of the power of Satan. Christ, as the Word of Wisdom, teaches the "recreated" person how to use the creation as God intended (p. 35).

Virginia Schurman describes the third stage in detail, as the original order of creation being restored through Christ, so that harmony, goodness and blessedness is restored together with right relationships throughout the creation (p. 36). This situation is the New Creation, and other creatures must be used sparingly, with respect, only when needed, and then for the glory of God .

Schurman's intepretation of Fox's writing is that he believed that humans were the stewards of creation, but it seems to me that it was more than stewardship that Fox was saying. Stewardship means looking after something for someone else, which would mean that the creation had no direct contact with God and is subordinate to humans.

Catherine Wilcox (1995) decribes the three stages similarly. She writes that some versions of the story give two stages, the old covenant and the new covenant, and some give four: from Adam to Moses, Moses, the prophets, and John the Baptist. She quotes William Smith, Burrough, Bayly, Charles Marshall and James Naylor who believed in these stages (p. 20). Wilcox's main theme is the ministry of women during the period, so she does not stress the value of references to the creation.

Looking at the writings of early Friends we see a consistency in their descriptions of the three stages of history, and the harmony obtaining in the last stage, as in the quotations below.

Francis Howgill (1618-1666) describes three stages, firstly the creation and its perfection: ... "All were subject in a sweet harmony, ... joy in heaven, peace on earth... The earth and all things were knit together in unity and harmony in one consent, as one family "(Hayes 1942 p. 85).

After the Fall "Unity lost with God and unity lost with every creature!" (p. 86). However, with the coming of Christ: "And then shall the Restorer be seen, who shall restore the earth into its first purity. Then shall the earth enjoy her rest, and the nations their sabbath" (p. 73).

Edward Burrough (1634-1662) writes similarly, (see the quotation in Chapter 5 p. 18) describing how the creatures became defiled when humans fell, but were restored with Christ's entry into the world.

Fox (1624-1691) describes these three stages and three teachers (Vol. 2, p.144,145). In the third stage he says that man and woman are renewed up to God's image, and so come into the state that man was in before he fell, and, Fox believes, into an even higher state.

In Fox's famous passage (Nickalls p. 27) he states that he felt as if he had entered paradise past the flaming swords of the angels set to keep the first humans out, that he was given an intuitive knowledge and wisdom of how to use the rest of creation and to live in harmony with it. In the last sentence he writes of "the hidden unity in the Eternal Being".

James Naylor (1618-1660) writes:

> And as man beholds the seed growing, so he comes to see the new creation, and what he lost in the Fall, and so is restored by the power of the word in the Son of God, into his dominion, power and purity, made able to resist the devil, to choose the thing that is good and delight in it, as before he delighted in the contrary; so comes man to be reconciled to his Maker in the eternal unity, beyond what is to be expressed. (1656 p. 52-53).

Isaac Pennington (1616-1681) is especially joyful:

> Is there not a new creation ? - a new heaven, a new earth; and are not all things become new therein ? Are not the old things of the night, and of the darkness, passed away, and all things become new in this day ?, which the Lord hath made, in the hearts which have received and been subject to his light? (*Works* Vol.3, p. 160).

James Parnell (1636-1656) was remarkable as he had such clear ideas at an early age. He wrote of the "world turned upside down" and wrote against hawking and hunting, saying that it was a sport for the rich and "devouring the creation"(Parnell 1675 p. 29). He believed that the Father is destroying the old creation and will "create new heavens and new earth wherein dwelleth rightousness; and there are the new creatures, in whom the new work is witnessed, in whom the Father hath manifested His son…" (Callaway 1846 p. 38).

William Penn (1644-1718), writing later, describes the creation:

> The World began in all innocency: all was then good that God had made: and he blessed the work of his hands, so their natures and harmony magnified him, their Creator. Then the morning stars sang together for joy, and all parts of his works said amen to his law. Not a jar in the whole frame; but man in paradise, the beasts in the field, the fowl in the air, the fish in the sea, the lights in the heavens, the fruits of the earth, yea the air, the earth, the water and fire, worshipped, praised and exalted his power, wisdom and goodness. O holy Sabbath, O holy day to the lord! (Penn 1825 p. 418,419).

Penn describes the fall as well but he does not continue with the restoration as do the others, perhaps because he was already beginning to realise that this paradise on earth was not actually being manifested. This must have stimulated his desire to found a new country where he could try to implement laws in accordance with the original vision.

Knowledge of the creation is mentioned by some writers, including Fox in his vision, and Thomas Lawson (1630-1691). Lawson writes that the Hebrew prophets and leaders knew by God's wisdom how to treat the creation, and lists Adam before he fell, Abraham, Moses, Solomon, Job and David as being "wise in the creation". (Lawson 1679 p. 4-11). Morries (2010) describes how this belief was lost in later years. It seems that they felt that this intuitive knowledge was God-given to those whose life was in the New Creation.

The New Creation was something very present for early Friends. They differed from the other sects of the time in believing that the New Creation had already come, and that human beings had the possibility of becoming new creatures. They therefore behaved accordingly, as if all people were equal, priests were not necessary, so tithes should not be paid, animals should be treated well, and God was everywhere, not only in churches. There was a living connection between God, the creation, and humans. This contrasted with others who were still expecting a millennium event and waiting in anticipation.

Early Friends also seem to have differed from others in their inclusion of the whole of creation in the "new creation". It was inclusive as they realised the importance of other species, which God had also created as well as humans. Theirs was therefore a holistic belief including all living things. Immediacy and unity were the hallmarks of early Friends beliefs about the whole of creation.

10

Linked with the new creation is the idea of a covenant between God and man, which man broke when in the Garden of Eden. The covenant involves certain pledges given by each of the parties to the other, not in a legal sense, but having something sacred about it. The word covenant occurs many times in the Bible, both in the Hebrew Bible, and also in the New Testament. Some of the references in the Hebrew Bible refer to the past and some to the new covenant which was to come. The Covenant of Life in particular mentions the whole of creation (Pickvance p. 63, 64).

Fox writes very early on:

> But people being strangers to the covenant of life with God, they eat and drink to make themselves wanton with the creatures, devouring them upon their own lusts and living in all filthiness, loving foul ways and devouring the creation; . ...(Nickalls p.2).

Howgill writes:

> ...and the Covenant of God will be established with you, in which you will receive the blessing in all things, and will know how to use all things to the glory of God (Hayes p. 73).

also

> Wait upon him who is given for a Covenant of Light, and Peace and Life, and all that receive this gift shall come to hear glad-tidings, peace on earth, and good-will (Hayes p. 65).

Burrough writes:

> The covenant of God is unity between God and man, and a binding each to another, to serve each other. The one is bound to obey, and submit, and worship; and the other to bless, and keep, and lead, and preserve (1672 p. 219).

Gwyn recognizes the connection to the whole of creation: "Fox knew a kind of covenantal integrity in his relationship to nature and to the word which created all things"(Gwyn 1995 p. 96).

> The covenant of creation and the covenant of redemption are thus one reality. The light's revelation gives new eyes that can no longer objectify gifts of nature as raw

commodities for the taking. Instead, one sees oneself as part of the whole covenantal web of relationships in nature and (a redeemed) culture (p. 118).
The created order complements and amplifies the knowledge of God in the heart. (p. 195).

The quotations above show that early Friends believed that in the third stage harmony is restored as it was in the beginning. The advent of Christ has brought the spirit of God into human beings, and even into the whole world. Humans thus became new beings, as the world became the New Creation. Humans are commanded to live in harmony with the rest of the creation. God, humans and the whole of creation are bound together, each with their own responsibilities and expectations.

It is rather fascinating to find that we can trace a connection to the "spiritual" group of the Fransicans in the 13th century, and have in common with them the practice of a simple life style and care for the whole of creation.

4. THE EVERLASTING GOSPEL AND GOSPEL ORDER

The new creation and the everlasting gospel are closely connected, but I have separated them here so as to concentrate on the link with gospel order . The origin of the myth of the three ages of history and the eternal gospel has been described in the last chapter. Hill (p.147, 148) uses both "Eternal" and "Everlasting" to describe the Gospel, but early Friends use the latter. I am assuming that they are the same thing. As the original term was in another language the translation could vary.

The meaning is given by Jones (*Studies...* p.173):

> I saw the angel of God, who flew into the middle of heaven, having the Eternal Gospel. This Gospel is called Eternal by John because that which Christ and the Apostles have given us is temporal and transitory so far as concerns the form of the sacraments, but eternal in respect to the truth which these signify.

Fox refers on a number of occasions to being sent to preach the everlasting gospel as when he says that that he was:

> sent to preach again the everlasting gospel, which had been preached before unto Abraham and in the apostles' days; and was to go over all nations and be preached to every creature (*Works* Vol 1 p. 304).

Again, Fox said he preached the everlasting gospel to be preached to all nations and to every creature (*Works,* Vol.1, pp 357 & 366), (see *Colossians 1.23*). On Firbank Fell Fox says that "the Lord had sent me with his everlasting gospel to preach..." (Nickalls p. 109). Fox interpreted the everlasting gospel as being the return of Christ to teach his people himself, and he travelled over the country preaching this gospel, gathering followers and other preachers as he went.

Burrough also writes about the everlasting gospel. His use of the word "fount" seems particularly significant:

> This gospel which is everlasting have we received from God and this is the fount of it which we give in the world unto the world for God and give glory to him, for the hour of his judgement is come and this is the everlasting gospel of salvation, he that can receive it, let him (1658 p. 16).

Pennington:

> These things are witnessed now again in the preaching of the same everlasting gospel by the same eternal spirit and power which preached it at first...
> (We) are required of him to proclaim the day of the Lord, the day of the Gospel, even the everlasting day which never shall have an end (*Works* Vol. 3 p. 495).

Hill writes that early Friends and others believed in the continous revelation of truth.

> Through revelation of new truths to believers, traditional Christianity could be adapted to the needs of a new age; the everlasting gospel *within* (my italics) responded more easily and swiftly to the pressures of the environment than did traditions of the church or the literal text. History is a gradual progress towards the total revelation of truth (J. Goodwin in Hill p. 367).

This seems to be a good summary of Quaker ideas, although not written by a Quaker.

Robert Barclay (Freiday 1967 p.103) also describes the everlasting gospel as being preached to all under the sun. However, he does not mention the origin of this idea, or the three stages of history, presumably aiming to make Quakerism respectable and avoid ideas which might be considered far fetched.

The concept of "gospel order" also arose from the everlasting gospel, as the extract below shows, written in 1668. It is rather a long quotation, but it seems to explain Fox's thoughts more clearly than trying to paraphrase them.

> The gospel order established amongst us is not of man nor by man but of and by Jesus Christ in and through the Holy Ghost. This order of the gospel which is from Christ the heavenly man, is above all the order of men... and will remain when they are gone. For the power of the gospel which is the everlasting gospel, was before the devil was, and will be and remain forever. And as the everlasting gospel was preached in the apostles' day to all nations, that all might come into the order of it through the divine power which brings life and immortality to light, that they who are heirs of it, might inherit the power and authority of it. These come to possess the joyful order of the joyful gospel, the comfortable order of the comfortable gospel, the glorious order of the glorious gospel and the everlasting order of the everlasting gospel, the power of God which will last forever...
> These shall see the government of Christ, who hath all power in heaven and earth given to him...
> (*Works* Vol 2 p. 80).

Fox also says that the gospel was the power of God which was preached before Matthew, Mark, Luke and John were written, and that it was preached to every creature, whether or not they ever saw the four gospels, so that every creature (human) was to obey the power of God (Vol 2 p. 20). This was written in 1663, quite early in Fox's development of the idea. It shows that Fox was a universalist, not limiting his ideas to the Christian faith. Three of Fox's Pastoral Letters, all written in 1674 refer to the connection between the everlasting gospel and gospel order (T. Canby Jones p.303, 306, 307, 309).

Fox was able to transform this idea into practical terms by setting up the structure of governance or order. It was thus not just an ideal, but an organised system which was to last indefinitely.

Gospel order has perhaps three main components: the enabling structure, the process of holding meetings, and the cosmic aspect, linking the gospel or human order to God and the order of nature.

Some writers emphasise the need to bring somewhat individualistic Friends into community, with the necessary discipline of subjection to the discernment of the group under Christ. This can be said to be a stage in this effort to bring Friends together, the letter from Balby elders being the start (1656) and the episode of Naylor triggering the second. Richard Farnsworth's epistle of 1666 signed by twelve leading (male) Friends stated the primacy of corporate Quaker authority over individual spiritual leadings and Fox followed it up when he came out of prison in Sept.1666 (Gwyn 1998 p.131).

The "settling" (Fox's term) of meetings is described in detail by Braithwaite (1921 p. 251 et seq.). It was a lengthy process, building on what had already been started, and consolidating the work, settling more meetings strategically situated throughout the country, fixing regular times of meetings, what should be considered, and who should attend.

The place of women was an important part of gospel order. Fox believed that men and women were "helpsmeets" in the image of God before they fell, but after the Fall the man was to rule over his wife. With the restoration by Christ, into the image of God and his righteousness and holiness again, man and women became helpsmeets as they were before the Fall (Braithwaite p. 273 from an epistle by Fox).

Separate women's meetings were established with their own field of work. Women were able to attend the other meetings, but were presumably always a minority and may not have been able to participate freely. Some meetings were limited to minsters or to "seasoned" Friends only.

The process of holding meetings meant that they were to regard Christ as their head, so that decisions were to be taken under Christ and not by humans alone.

For Fox it seems to have been a natural progression from preaching the gospel to gathering Friends together under Christ to become a community (Benson 1976) for group spiritual discernment. This was designed to unite Friends and minimise too much individualism which might go outside the order of the gospel.

There was more than a disciplinary reason for gospel order, however, as Fox was clear that Christ was the head of the meeting, and his direct government by the Spirit was the Gospel Order (Gwyn 1998 p.131). The setting up of the meetings was the instrument by which Christ's rule could be instituted.

The everlasting gospel seems to connect to the following passage mentioned by Freiday in his reponse to Schurman (p. 46). He quotes one of Lewis Benson's Rolodex notes to himself under the heading "Gospel Order", which reads:

Fox connects the Gospel Order with the Restoration of all things by Christ. The Gospel Order is therefore not merely Apostolic and Primitive, but has *cosmic* properties (emphasis added). In the Gospel Order, and not outside of it, man fulfills the original purpose for which he was created...

This seems to refer to the everlasting gospel and the coming of the new creation, so restoring peace and harmony.

Wilson elaborates on the cosmic aspects (Wilson p. 3). He writes that Gospel Order:

is the order established by God that exists in every part of creation...It is the right relationship of every part of creation, however small, to every other part and to the Creator. Gospel order is the harmony and order which God established at the moment of creation, and which enables the individual aspects of creation to achieve that quality of being which God intended from the start, about which God could say "It was very good.

The connection to the whole creation is an important aspect of Gospel Order, linking man, God and the creation in a harmonious whole. The cosmos was seen to have its own order, designed by God, and so connects with the order for humans under Christ.

5. ANIMALS

The Lord showed me...and that I might not eat and drink to make myself wanton but for health, using the creatures in their service, as servants in their places, to the glory of him that hath created them; they being in their covenant and I being brought up into the covenant, as sanctified by the Word which was in the beginning, by which all things are upheld; wherein is unity with the creation.
But people being strangers to the covenant of life with God, they eat and drink to make themselves wanton with the creatures, devouring them upon their own lusts, and living in all filthiness, loving foul ways and devouring the creation; and all in this world, in the pollutions thereof, without God; and therefore I was to shun all such. (*Works* Vol. 1 p. 68).

So George Fox writes that this was shown to him when he was eleven, which is a remarkable insight for someone of that age.

Fox packs a great deal into this paragraph: that the creatures (note 4) should only be used for health, to the glory of God, that they have their covenant and their place, as Fox has his covenant, and he seems to refer to the Garden of Eden where there was unity in the creation. The creatures have their own covenant as in *Hosiah* 2.18.

> And in that day will I make a covenant for them with the beasts of the field, and with the fowls of the heaven, and with the creeping things of the ground: and I will break the bow and the sword and the battle out of the earth, and will make them to lie down safely.

God also makes a covenant with humans and all living things after the flood (*Genesis* 9 v. 9-10 and 15).

In Fox's vision of "the paradise of God", he says that

> ...it was showed me how all things had their names given them according to their nature and virtue. And I was at a stand in my mind whether I should practice physic for the good of mankind, seeing the nature and virtue of the creatures were so opened to me by the Lord (*Works* Vol. 1 p. 85).

He believes that those presuming to be physicians did not really know the true value of nature as shown to him (Fox) by God. There are a number of other passages in Fox's writings about the lack of the wisdom of God of the "physicians", but also how they could be reformed and could learn to understand the virtues of the creatures (*Works* Vol 1 p. 85, 86). These passages occur in a section in which Fox is stating that "physic", divinity and the law were all out of the wisdom, the faith and the justice of God, but they could all be reformed by being brought into the true faith, the law and the wisdom of God.

Later, in 1657, in Dorset Fox writes that he drew up some queries for the "mountebanks" (itinerant quack doctors):

> In the evening we drew up some queries concerning the ground of all diseases, and the natures and virtues of medicinable creatures, and sent them to the mountebanks, letting them know, 'if they would not answer we would stick them on the cross the next day'
> (*Works* Vol 1 p. 323).

Here Fox stresses the need to rely on the wisdom of God to understand the creatures and how they should be used. He claims that he has received this wisdom directly from God. This links with his belief that it was not necessary to go to Oxford or Cambridge to know the word of God. So he also believes that he has the power of healing due to direct insights from God of the value of nature.

In one of his epistles Fox writes:

> Wait all in the light for the wisdom by which all things were made, with it to use all the Lord's creatures to his glory, (and none to stumble one another about the creatures, for that is not from the light), for which end they were created, and with the wisdom by which they were made, ye may be kept out of the misuse of them, in the image of God, that ye may come to see, that "the earth is the Lord's and the fullness thereof and the earth may come to yield her increase, and to enjoy her Sabbaths;... (Fox *Works* Vol .7 p. 40).

Fox urges people to "wait in the light" for the wisdom as to how to behave, and here he shows a holistic view of the earth and all its creatures.

Fox put his principles into practice, as is mentioned on two occasions in his Journal, once when (probably in Aberystwyth) he saw the man who was supposed to be looking after his horse filling his own pockets. Fox writes that he was wicked and thievish to rob a poor dumb creature, and he would rather he had robbed him (Nickalls p. 301).

On another occasion Fox was being taken to prison in Lancaster and was set upon a "poor little horse" which they led by a halter. When they left the town they beat the horse and made him kick and gallop. Fox got off and told them that they should not abuse the creature, "at which they mightily raged"(Nickalls p. 376).

Fox objected to people using animals for sport, glorying in their own power, and causing the animals gratuitous suffering.

Edward Burrough (*Works* p. 251) refers to the three stages, the Creation, the Fall, and the Restoration. He links the corruption of humans with that of the animals, believing that the latter were affected by the behavior of man, as in the following quotation:

> All creatures that God hath made, in their creation and beginning were very good in his sight that made them, and until man that was to use them, and no creature was evil or defiled in its creation. But man, transgressing against his Maker, became evil in the sight of the Lord; being

possessed with evil and corrupted, makes all creatures evil in the exercise of them, corrupts them, and perverts them to another end wherefore they were created.

But man being restored and redeemed, and renewed again into covenant with God, through the condemning of the evil, then all creatures are restored to him and made blessed.

Francis Howgill says something similar. (See Chapter 3 p. 8).

This feeling of kinship with the whole of creation resulted in practical actions and writings against some of the cruelties of the day, such as bull baiting. James Naylor and Thomas Taylor (1617-1682) both write about these so called sports. James Naylor writes that after he had been moved to go to Chesterfield in l655 he heard a great noise outside the house he was in and discovered that there was bull baiting going on. He was much troubled in spirit, but waited to know the will of God and whether he should go in and declare against their unGodly practice. However, after he had waited a short time he was moved to write to the man they call their teacher (i.e. the Puritan minister) so as to lay the matter before him, as the people indulging in the baiting knew no better. Naylor objected to the baiting, not because it gave pleasure to the spectators but because it was "setting one of the creatures of God against another to torment." (Damrosch p. 245).

There are at least three passages in Thomas Taylor's writings against bear and bull baiting and other cruel "sports". For example:

> And all ye that can pleasure yourselves with beholding one Creature hurt and torment another yea, and sometimes even unto death as at Bull-baitings, Bear-baitings, Cock-fightings and the like. O! what minds have ye, and how contrary are ye to the Tender nature of Christ and all Christians truly called, who could never rejoice in any such things, by reason of tender, pitiful and merciful Nature! O ye children of cruelty! when will your Hearts break, your stony Hearts melt into tears before the lord for your mighty sins? And when will you bring your Deeds to the Light, that ye may see the ugliness of your sins, and repent of them... (1697 p. 128-9).

In the same book Taylor has other passages, one "To the Bearward" condemning bear-baiting as being lewd and wicked, contrary to the law of God and the Nation (p. 62). Another passage "A Testimony against Bull and Bear-baiting" is to the magistrates of Stafford, saying that to delight in seeing bulls, bears and dogs tearing and tormenting one another without cause is a grievous sin in the Sight of God. Also that is "does great hurt to the minds of your young ones who are led away from remembering their Creator..." (p. 159).

The list of offences punishable under "Laws Agreed upon in England" for Pennsylvania included "bull baiting, cockfighting and the like, which excite the people to rudeness, cruelty, looseness and irreligion". (Beatty p.291)

This holistic and inspired belief of the unity of animals with humans was held for a fairly brief period, as later, though Friends were kind to animals, they lost the depth of religious belief which carried them forward and transformed their lives.

Collective statements came later. In 1698 Aberdeen MM records:

> amongst men we condemn all shooting with guns of any sort for game or recreation; all shooting with bows and arrows... also we condemn all hunting with dogs and hawking, as altogether unsuitable to that weighty testimony God hath called us unto. (Braithwaite 1961 p. 513).

In the minutes of Leinster Province inquiry is to be made what Friends keep greyhounds or hunting dogs. (Braithwaite 1961, p. 510) The emphasis here is on the unsuitability of such sport for Friends, rather than any cruelty it involves, and shows the gradual loss of vision which is replaced by a concern for respectability.

In these minutes one denotes a switch from the compassion for animals and feelings of unity with them to a concentration on the effects on humans of such sports, making them less able to do God's work. Such thoughts are not mentioned by Fox, Burrough or Howgill, who write more of rejoicing in the whole of creation and being in unity with it.

The care for other creatures was carried on in the 18th Century by American Friends, in particular John Woolman, Joshua Evans and Anthony Benezet, but this will not be dealt with here. However, I will just mention the writings of others about Quakers, although they are also of a later date.

When one looks at the views of non-Quakers one finds that the kindness to animals of Quakers stood out, as noted by Thomas Clarkson and also Lewis G. Regenstein. Clarkson worked with Quakers in the 18th Century in efforts to abolish the slave trade and writes that he got to know them well. He devotes several pages in his "Portraiture of Quakerism" to a very sympathetic account of Friends' treatment of animals. He explains the "New Covenant" under which men develop a love for animals and will treat them with tenderness. He explains that Quakers view animals not as brute machines, but as a creation of God. Duties towards animals arise from a spiritual feeling, their strengths, capacities and feelings should be considered, as well as their ability to feel pain. He also writes about Quaker objections to "diversions of the field" which include hunting, and also racing and cockfighting. Clarkson writes that Quakers look after their companion animals well and behave as if they were their guardians (1807 p.179-81). In fact, Clarkson, though not a Quaker, seems to have greater insight into what early Friends believed than some later Quaker writers.

Regenstein writes that when the Quaker movement was founded English humanitarians gained an important ally in their 22 year long struggle to enact animal protection legislation. He says that at that time England was the scene of some of the most brutal public "entertainments" involving the torture of animals, usually undertaken with the approval and often the participation of the church (p. 86).

The tender feeling for animals was based on the vision of the restoration of unity in the creation and the belief that animals were valued by God and had their own part to play. However, though Quakers remained generally kind to animals, in the next century the reason for this kindness was obscured. The vision of unity was lost or underplayed.

6. EDUCATION

Early Friends were very aware of the value of education. However, they disagreed with the syllabus obtaining at the time, and they tried to set up their own schools where ever it seemed possible. Like many of the sects they did not hold that education should centre on the classics, and tried to introduce more practical subjects into the curriculum. Other subjects were religion, especially the Bible, ethical conduct, nature, and "whatsoever is useful in the creation".

I have drawn from the writings of four early Friends in this chapter: Fox, Thomas Lawson (1630-1691), Penn, and John Bellers (1624-1725), all of whom wrote about the value of education, and on the whole have similar views about it. They all mention the natural world and the value of our relationship with it, practical subjects, and the moral aspects.

In methods of teaching, as well as in subjects taught, Quakers differed from the Puritan view that children were naturally sinful and should be strictly controlled and their natural impulses curbed. Believing in the divine spirit in each child led them to lay more emphasis on careful training and the encouragement of finding out the truth for themselves, and of making moral choices instead of the strict discipline enforced by the Puritans (Loukes p. 89).

The quotations below largely concur in their views:

George Fox, quite early in his Journal (1649) records:

> I was much exercised with school-masters and school mistresses, warning them to teach their children sobriety in the fear of the lord, that they might not be nursed and trained up in lightness, vanity and wantonness. Likewise I was made to warn masters and mistresses, fathers and mothers in private families, to take care that their children and servants might be trained in the fear of the lord; that they themselves should be therein examples and patterns of sobriety and virtue to them... ought to train up their children in the new covenant of light, Christ Jesus, who is God's salvation to the ends of the earth, that all may know their salvation. And they ought to train them up in the law of life, the law of the Spirit, the law of love and of faith, that they might be made free of the law of sin and death... (*Works* Vol 1, p. 93).

Even earlier than the above (1646), Fox writes:

> the Lord opened to me that being bred at Oxford or Cambridge was not enough to fit and qualify men to be ministers of Christ: and I wondered at it, because it was the common belief of people (*Works,* Vol 1 p. 71).

Later (1658) Fox met a man from London who wanted to set up a college in Durham to make ministers of Christ, but Fox and others reasoned with him, telling him that Christ's disciples were able to preach without the knowledge of Latin and Greek, and it seems the man was dissuaded from his project. (*Works.* Vol 1 p. 362).

In those days, with no state education, it was possible to start small schools wherever the conditions seemed favourable. In 1668 Fox returning towards London by Waltham "advised the setting up of a school there for teaching boys; and also a women's school to be opened at Shacklewell for instructing girls and young maidens in whatsoever things were civil and useful in the creation". (*Works,* Vol 2 p. 74.) This shows that Fox was concerned with the education of girls as well as boys, which was unusual in those days. He also emphasises the value of education, not just to the individual but to the whole community, "in the creation".

Fox was given a grant of land in Pennsylvania by Penn in 1681, part of which he planned to use for a meeting house, school house and botanic garden, but this did not materialise (Nickalls p. 754).

These quotations show the seriousness with which Fox took education, and that it should have an emphasis on moral behaviour, on the need of the knowledge of Christ, and the natural world, rather than classical languages. He emphasises the new covenant, proclaiming the love of God, as opposed to the fear which was emphasised by the Puritans.

Thomas Lawson was a teacher and had a university education, involving the classics. However, in his two books, *Dagons Fall* (1679) and *A Mite into the Treasury* (1680) he emphasises practical subjects. He writes in the first that it was "written primarily as a testimony for the Lord, his Wisdom, Creation, Products of his Power, Useful and Necessary Knowledge, Capacitating People for the Concerns of this Life."(Lawson 1679 p. 1).

> Secondarily: as a Testimony against the Old Serpent, his wisdom which is Foolishness with God, His Arts, Invention, Comedies, or Interluds, Tragedies, Lascivious Poems, Frivolus Fables, Spoiling Philosophy taught in Christian Schools." (Lawson p. 73).

> But being that all savoury and sound knowledge related primarily to God, secondarily to the Knowledge of the Creation, and of the useful and necessary Imployment. My Testimony is that children should be instructed in the aforesaid in the fear of the Lord, it being the Door of Heavenly Wisdom. (Lawson p. 88).

The subjects he suggests include rules for gardening, agriculture, cattle, building, navigation, medecine, law, improvement of lands, bees, propagation of plants, and various other useful skills. He stresses the need for "knowledge of the Lord, of His Creation, and of necessary and useful things whereby they might be qualified for the help, benefits and advantages of others, in their respective Generations ...." (p. 62).

In support of his ideas Lawson quotes the Waldenses, Albigensies and Bohemians, who did not study at universities, and most of whose ministers were tradesmen (p. 88), and states that Wycliff, Hus and Luther amongst others distrusted the work of the universities.

Lawson also relates, in 1691:

> Some years ago, George Fox, William Penn and others were concerned to purchase a piece of land near London for the use of a "Garden School-house and a dwelling house for the master, in which garden one or more of each sort of our English plants were to be planted, and also many outlandish (foreign) plants. My purpose was to write a book on these in Latin, so that as boy had the description

of these in book lessons and their virtues, he might see them growing in the garden or plantation, to gain knowledge of them... Subjects were to be God Himself, the book of life and the book of creation: and they that grow up in the knowledge of the Lord and of His creation, they are the true philosophers... His work within and His works without, even the least of plants, preaches forth the power and the wisdom of the Creator; and, eyed in the spark of eternity, humbles man. (Braithwaite 1921, p. 528).

Regarding the whole of creation, Lawson writes that the Book of Life and the Book of Creation should be sufficient for all educational requirements.

Lawson had the belief that the early Hebrew characters had an intuitive understanding of nature. Adam, Moses, Solomon, Job and others knew the virtues of living creatures, plants, stones and other minerals. This he believed is essential inward knowledge, not from books, but by "passive reception of Divine things, not by study, but by patience and submission" (p. 54). This was a belief shared by others of the time, and it is interesting to speculate how it compares with his careful scientific botanising in his later years when he travelled all over England recording his finds.

The above quotations show that Lawson was primarily concerned to teach about God, the Creation, and useful subjects which would help not only the learner, but others as well. This contrasted with the system then practiced, of teaching the classics, literature, logic, mathematics, music, and other subjects, which he felt were of no use unless linked to spiritual understanding, and of some practical value, both to the learner and to others who might be helped thereby,

William Penn (1825) has some clear and, even today, advanced ideas about education. He devotes a section of one of his books to education, under numbered points:

> 8. Children had rather be making of tools and instruments of play; shaping, drawing, framing and building etc., than getting some rules of propriety of speech.
> 9. It were happy if we studied nature more in natural things; and acted according to nature; whose rules are few, plain, and most reasonable.
> 10. Let us begin where she begins, go her place, and close always where she ends, and we cannot miss of being good naturalists. (p. 354).

There is a long passage of 17 points on education with the main emphasis on studying nature, as this is where one can see "the stamp of its Maker". People would be less likely to abuse the natural world if they knew more about it and saw God in every part. He extols the beauty of the countryside and all that God has provided for humans and states that they are the servants to care for the creation.

> 223. The country is both the philosopher's garden and library, in which he reads and contemplates the power, wisdom and goodness of God.
> 224. It is his food, as well as study; and gives him life aswell as learning (p. 371).

Penn had a great feeling for the care of the creation:

> 13. For how could men find the conscience to abuse it, while they should see the great Creator look them in the face, in all and every part thereof ?
> 14. Therefore ignorance makes them insensible, and that insensibility may be ascribed to their hard useage of several parts of this noble creation that has the stamp and voice of DEITY everywhere, and in everything to the observing (p. 354-355).

Penn goes on to describe the value of study of the natural world in schools and for gardeners and husbandmen, to help them appreciate its wonder.

In a letter to his wife in 1682 on leaving England for Pennsylvania he wrote, regarding the education of the children:

> Let it be useful knowledge, in such as is consistent with Truth and godliness... the useful parts of mathematics, as building houses or ships, measuring, surveying, dialling, navigation... agriculture.. let my children be husbandmen and housewives... This leads to consider the works of God and nature, of things that are good, and diverts the mind from being taken up with the vain arts and inventions of a luxurious world... Be sure to observe their genius and do not cross it as to learning; let them not dwell too long on one thing, but let their change be agreeable, and all their diversions have some little bodily labour in them. (Braithwaite 1921 p. 529).

Here Penn advises on the method of education as well as the content.

Penn's writing and his vision of education is inspirational and it is sad that so little, if any, of it was put into practice. He emphasises the relationship of God to the whole creation and the need to learn the intricacies of the natural world and to work in harmony with nature rather than exploiting it without knowledge. He was writing when it had probably been realised that the "new Creation" was not going to materialise, so it was necessary to plan for a continuation of the present situation. This would have made him especially keen to establish a type of government which would put into practice Quaker ideals.

Penn also emphasises the value of letting children develop their own interests and not to pressurise them or keep them too long at one task. All of the above seems useful contemporary advice.

John Bellers agreed with Penn and Lawson that children should be taught useful subjects as well as reading and writing. He advocated setting up institutions called "Colledges" instead of workhouses, where all sorts of useful learning could be taught. There should be a library, a physick garden for understanding of herbs, and a laboratory for preparing medecines. He envisaged people from other countries coming who would teach their own languages. He believed that even the poor and deprived are capable of development, given the right opportunities. This idea was very similar to Robert Owen's promotion of "Villages of Co-operation" over a hundred years later. Beller's ideas are elaborated in George Clarke's valuable compendium (1987 p. 44).

The interest of early Quakers in education concerning the whole of creation comes out in the above writings. In some ways their ideas were similar to those of other sects, and writers such as Winstanley, in wanting more practical education. However, the earliest were also aware of the advent of the New Creation where all were equal and the rest of creation was part of a holistic system.. They were educating for a new world where all living things lived in harmony. There was a new covenant with God, which was in contrast to the Puritan covenant of fear. Penn's writing is particularly interesting in his desire to co-operate with nature, rather than exploiting her and shows a vision for the future from which we could well learn.

Braithwaite states that "It is possible, if circumstances had allowed, Friends might have developed a great system of "natural" education, which would have been of wide service to the country" (1921 p. 530). Sadly, towards the end of the century and in the 18th century education became "guarded", with an emphasis on outward conformity, and the spiritual fervour of the early "Publishers of Truth" was largely lost (p. 536). However, we can look back to the early pioneers for inspiration and guidance.

7. PRAISE POEMS

Thus in part I have shewed unto you the state of the earth,
and of mankind, and the glory of God's creation, and the
blessedness thereof; but if I should declare unto the whole

world from year's end to year's end, I should fall short, and words would be wanting, to express the felicity and happiness in which man was brought forth.

So Francis Howgill (Hayes p. 74) writes in joy and thankfulness.

Inspite of their imprisonments and brutal persecution, and the time they spent writing journals, tracts, and answers to their opponents, early Friends took time to write in praise of God's work in the whole of creation. It is as if they were overwhelmed by the beauty around them and recognised that it was all a gift from God. They also believed that this gift must only be used for the glory of God and not wantonly. They were steeped in the Bible, so that echoes of it can be heard in many of their writings, taken into their hearts and not just parotted. Two passages from George Fox's writings show these beliefs:-

The first is from a letter to Friends in New England, Virginia and Barbados, written in 1672:

> He is the living God that clothes the earth with grass and herbs, and causes the trees to grow, and bring forth food for you, and makes the fishes of the sea to breathe and live, and makes the fowls of the air to breed, and causes the roe and the hind, and the creatures, and all the beasts of the earth to bring forth, whereby they may be food for you.
> He is the living God, that causes the stars to arise in the night, to give you light, and the moon to be a light in the night.
> He is the living God that causes the sun to give warmth to you, to nourish you when you are cold.
> He is the living God that causes the snow and frost to melt, and causes the rain to water the plants.
> He is the living God, that made the heaven and the earth, and the clouds, and causes the springs to break out of the rocks, and divided the great sea from the earth, and divided the light from the darkness, by which it is called day, and the darkness night, and divided the great waters from the earth, and gathered them together: which great waters he called sea, and the dry land earth; he is to be worshipped that doth this.
> He is the living God that gives unto you breath and life, and strength, and gives unto you beasts and cattle, whereby you may be fed and clothed.
> He is the living God and he is to be worshipped.
> (*Works* Vol. 8, p. 42).

This was originally written as prose, but I have separated the lines as when read aloud it sounds like a poem.

Fox also felt that, as God is the Lord of all, all of creation would praise him, not just humankind. So he writes, in a tract called "Good morrow and good even":

> ...such as are turned to the Light which comes from him who is the Heir of all things, which upholds all things by his word and power, these come to see how all the works of the Lord praise him; his works praise him, day and night praise him, Summer and Winter praise him; Ice and Cold, and Snow praise him;... Seed-time and Harvest praise him; and all things that are created praise him. This is the Language of them who learn of him; hear him that is Heir of all things, who upholds all things by his Word and power, by whom all things was made, and by whom all things was created for him, and to him, that above all things he might have the preheminence. (1657 p. 12).

Edward Burrough writes:

> The true God is a spirit, and is infinite, eternal and everlasting, the Creator of all things, the life and being of all things, the power by which all things stand. All creatures have a being in him, and by him, and without him no creature is, or doth move upon the face of the earth. This is he whom we worship, and fear, and obey (1672 p. 241).

James Naylor writes:

> When I look back into thy works I am astonished and see no end of thy praises: glory, glory, to thee, saith in my soul, and let my heart be ever filled with thanksgiving; whilst thy works remain, they shall show forth thy Power.
> Then didst thou lay the foundation of the Earth and ledst me under the waters, and in the deep didst thou show me wonders, and thy Forming of the world. By thy Hand thou led me in safety till thou showdst me the pillars of the earth; then did the heavens shower down: they was covered with darkness and the powers thereof was shaken, and thy glory descended; thou filled the lower parts of the earth with gladness, and the springs of the valleys were opened; thy showers descended abundantly, so the earth was filled with virtue. Thou made thy plants to spring, and the thirsty soul became as a watered garden... (*Works* p. 268, 9).

This was printed in the year (1659) that Naylor was released from his three-year imprisonment, before which he had been severely whipped, branded with a red hot iron, and had his tongue bored through. It could have been written before this excessive punishment, but if it was written after this it shows the great courage of his spirit.

Francis Howgill writes rather similarly:

> Beauty, Beauty! Glory, glory!
> Eternity, eternity! Almightiness, almightiness!
> Power, Riches, Honour, Dignity and Dominion!
> Strength, Wisdom and Goodness!
> Fulness, Satisfaction, Eternal Treasure,
> Durable Riches,
> Infiniteness is his Name forever!
> Unexpressively I am filled with his Love and Power
> He opens the Windows of Heaven
> He rains his showers as silver drops
> And as fine myrrh, as sweet odours.
> He nourishes the young;
> He carries the Lambs in his Arms of Love;
> He drives gently them that are with young;
> He is true and faithful forever;
> He keeps Covenant;
> He is long suffering and kind.
> Who can declare his Power
> I am lost in the incomprehensible Being of Eternal
> Love.
> (Hayes p. 45, 46).

This also was not written as a poem in the original.

Thomas Taylor takes great delight in the creation:

> Hear O Earth, and hearken ye heavens, for the Lord hath spoken, even the Lord God mighty in Power and excellent wisdom...
> ...And if this is the Mountain of God's House and Holiness indeed, which is now on the top of all Mountains; and here the Lord is fully seen, and his living power daily felt, and his everlasting love continually enjoyed, for watering and refreshing the Babes and Living Plants of the New Jerusalem; glory, glory for ever, glory to the righteous, for this is comely... (1660).

These poems show a great thankfulness and appreciation of God's bounty and his love, in contrast to the Puritan beliefs of a stern and possibly punitive God. They were written at about the same time as Henry Vaughan, Andrew Marvell and Thomas Traherne, but the Quaker poems are outpourings of thanksgiving, not especially crafted.

William Penn is more prosaic in his expression, but he is also very conscious of the gifts of God:

> 484. The world represents a rare and sumptuous palace, mankind the great family in it; and God, the mighty Lord and Master of it.
> 485. We are all sensible what a stately seat it is: the heavens adorned with so many glorious luminaries; and the earth with groves, plain, valleys, hills, fountains, ponds, lakes and rivers; and a variety of fruits, and creatures for food, pleasure and profit. In short, how noble a house he keeps, and the plenty, and variety, and excellency of his table: his order and seasons, and suitableness of every time and thing. But we must be as sensible, or at least ought to be, what careless and idle servants we are, and how short and disproportionate our behaviour is to his bounty and goodness: how long he bears, how often he reprieves and forgives us, who, not withstanding our breach of promises, and repeated neglects, has not yet been provoked to break up house, and send us to shift for ourselves. Should not this great goodness raise a due sense in us of our undutifulness, and a resolution to alter our course, and mend out manners, that we may be for the future more worthy communicants at our Master's good and great table...
> 486. But though God has replenished this world with abundance of good things for man's comfort, yet they are all but imperfect goods. He is the only perfect good to whom they point. But, alas, men cannot see him for them; though they should always see him in them." (1825 p. 387).

Like other Friends, and Fox in particular, Penn is very much aware of the selfishness and greed with which so many people use the gifts of God. The above passage may well have been influenced by his aquisition of Pennsylvania and his hopes for its colonisation by hard working and thrifty Friends who would not despoil the relatively untouched countryside.

Early Friends were mostly rural people, the majority being involved in agriculture, but they did not take the countryside for granted. They seemed continually aware of its beauty, and they were deeply grateful to God for all his gifts.

Though they resemble hymns in some ways, these writings were not meant to be sung in a congregation, but were outpourings from full hearts. Worship was based on silence and spontaneous spoken words, rather than anything previously prepared.

8. THE FADING OF THE VISION

The clear vision of the early pioneers gradually faded, especially towards the end of the century. This was for a number of reasons. For one thing, historically, the "Age of Reason" was slowly replacing the "Age of the Spirit" (Cragg 1970). New discoveries in science encouraged people to look with scepticism at some of the religious idealism of earlier in the century. Science promoted industry, which encouraged commerce, and economics came to play a more important role. Reason was stressed, rather than faith, intuition and feeling. The writings of Bacon, Descartes and others emphasised the importance of humans and their right to dominate the rest of creation.

Quakers were not immune to these influences. Many Friends went into business, being denied university education, and though they were often benevolent employers, care for the creation itself was not generally apparent in their work.

In accordance with the "spirit of the age" the writings of Fox and others were edited by a committee, some twenty years after his death, consequently: "it was thought wise not only to omit or tone down many passages which to a politer age might seem wild or fanatical, but to smooth out Fox's rugged style and occasionally outlandish vocabulary" (Nuttall in Nickalls p. xxx). Similarly Thomas Ellwood commented on Lawson's writings, that some of his phrases were "a little uncouth", and his visions "likely to amaze rather than benefit a reader." (Whittaker 1986, p. 1).

According to Gwyn (1998 p. 134) after 1666 Fox forged new alliances with wealthier and better placed Friends. Quakerism became redefined as a "coherent and respectable doctrinal system". So it was no longer a threat to the established order.

Barclay's Apology, published in 1676, attempted to codify Quakerism and at the same time, make it more acceptable to the changing times. Gwyn (1998 p. 135) writes that Barclay presented a Quaker theology within a Puritan framework, so losing the vision and enthusiasm of early Friends. Barclay's main reference to creation is about how it should be used by humans, and he concludes that "those who have abundant possessions, and are accustomed to such things by education, may make better use of them without extravagance or waste than those who are unaccustomed to them or do not have the capacity to utilize them". (Freiday 1967, p. 392). Barclay was anxious to reassure those who might suspect that Quakerism had some "levelling" propensities, and believed that someone who had been dispensed with more of God's creation than others should use it for "his own good, that of his brethren and to the glory of God" (Freiday 1967, p. 392). However, he also says that those who have plenty should be willing to help those who are in need, but those who have less should be content with their lot. This seems a long way from the ideals of Fox and other early Friends.

Rufus Jones was considerably upset by "The Apology" and by its lack of recognition of the revelatory experiences of early Friends. He writes that Barclay was attempting to fit Quakerism to the doctrines of the Reformation, but ignored the experiences of the mystics (Jones 1921, p. xxxii – xli). Barclay had adjusted Quakerism to fit in with "the Augustinian and Calvinistic system, instead of following the fresh and transforming path which the spiritual reformers, the real forerunners and progenitors of the Children of Light had discovered". Jones writes that Barclay altered the entire character of the Quaker movement, and its mysticism shifted from the dynamic affirmation mysticism of the first period to a passive and negative type, so that "Quietism" settled down upon it and utterly transformed it. Jones devotes some 15 pages to this heartfelt feeling.

Friends became concerned with the minutia of dress, furnishings of their houses, rules about "disownment", marriage procedure and other internal behaviour, and lost the outgoing mission to the whole world. Instead of feeling that Quakerism was a vision for all, they shrank into a small group, perhaps showing an example, but only for the elect few.

The apocalyptic vision, the new creation and the everlasting gospel were also lost, and with it the idea of the restoration of harmony between God, humans and the whole of creation. Later Quaker writers took their cue from Barclay and rarely mention the early vision. This, to my mind, is a great loss, as the only way we can understand the witness and testimonies of Quakers is by accepting the vision as a whole.

9. DISCUSSION

This discussion will include three aspects of the experience of early Friends: firstly, the "paradigm shift" which early Friends experienced in their lives; secondly, the feeling of unity to which this led, and thirdly, how the whole of creation was part of their vision.

Early Friends experienced a paradigm shift in their lives. All who were faithful could experience the same new life, so that a new community would be born in which there was peace and harmony with the rest of creation. It was a holistic vision, involving God, the whole of nature, and humans. The whole of creation, being created by God, was sacred. The experience of Fox (Nickalls p. 27) contains all three of these aspects: he came "up in spirit though the flaming sword", he came "to know the hidden unity in the Eternal Being" and "the creation was opened to him" so that he knew how "all things had their names given to them according to their nature and virtue". These quotes cover the pardigm shift, the feeling of unity, and the relationship with the rest of the creation.

32

This change of worldview came from the Bible itself, the idea that Christ had come to each his people himself, their apocalyptic vision, and in particular, their beliefs about the third stage of history and the everlasting gospel. They write as if they were inspired by the idea of the newness, freshness and hope of a new world in which there would be peace and harmony between all of creation, as there had been in paradise. Several modern writers including Wilson and Keiser describe these changes.

What such a paradigm shift entailed is described by Wilson (p. 16) as being similar to the drawings in introductory textbooks on psychology which can be seen in two ways, such as a dark vase or two light faces facing one another. Depending on how you look at them you can see either interpretation. Keiser's description of the New Creation describes a similar change in consciousness:

> ...the New Creation is the world in its depths. Beneath our surface life the world exists in our depths as originally created. While obscured in the Fall, it has not been obliterated. The Light opens us to our depths and there we are brought into touch with the original matrix of our being. (p.5).

This paradigm shift involved a feeling of unity with God and with the whole of creation. Unity with the creation was a fundamental theme amongst early Friends, as Fox, Howgill, Burrough and others write. As described in Chapter 2, this was part of the general belief of the time, but expressed particularly clearly by early Friends.

Wilson also brings in the theme of unity, writing that Quakerism is a "gestalt" i.e. a whole, with each part closely related to each other: "an integrated structure or pattern that makes up all of experience and has specific properties that can neither be derived from the elements of the whole nor considered simply as the sum of these elements." (p. 16). So Quakerism is more than the sum of its parts, and has to be considered as a whole.

R. Melvin Keiser's pamphlet is "a theological meditation on the centre and circumference of Quakerism". He writes that "The centre of Quakerism is the Inward Light, its circumference the New Creation" (p. 3). "To respond to the Light is to come into unity not only with God but with the world." (p. 5). So he writes that "God and the world are inseparable because we relate inherently both to the divine presence acting on each of us and to the web of interrelations in the world within which we dwell." (p.3). Also:

> Beneath our sinful experience of a distorted world is the illumined experience of the world in its original freshness and power permeated by divine presence. The redeemed life is to dwell in unity with God and the world, knowing the

true nature of creatures through a felt unity with them in God, and to act in accord with that unity" (p. 15).

Gwyn also takes this view: "Fox taught that not only did the rich exploit the poor but they also "devoured the creatures" through conspicuous consumption. Hence the imperative to a simple life style was a call to solidarity with the earth as well as fellow humanity." (1998 p. 12).

To feel in unity with God and with creation results in a totally different way of relating to the world and to other species. It gives a sense of security, but also of awareness and feeling of being in touch with the cosmos, responsible for one's part in its evolution.

The quotations above, and the preceding chapters give evidence of both the paradigm shift, the feeling of unity, and the relationship with the whole of creation enjoyed by early Friends.

It is difficult for us to understand, let alone enter into the world of early Friends. It seems to me that the new creation was fundamental to early Friends' experience. It was an experience rather than a vision, the feeling that the spirit of Christ had entered human beings, and also the whole of creation, so making new men and women as well as a new world. The shift of perspective regarding the whole of creation produced a new way of looking at the world. It was this experience which gave them the determination and courage to persist in their mission in spite of attacks by the general public and long periods of imprisonment under atrocious conditions which caused the death of many.

The writings show that early Friends had a close relationship to creation, and felt that God, the Creation and humans are all connected with one another, each having a part to play in the order of the universe. Friends were called to preach the everlasting gospel which stated the immanence of the new creation. God, humans and the creation are connected to one another by covenants, confirming the order of the Gospel, and the order in creation designed by God. The whole Creation is thus valued by God and not only of value to humans for what they can get from it. Humans must respect and work with the Creation, rather than being in a superior position. This means that we need to treat the rest of creation with care and consideration, recognising our relationship with it through God and our relationship to God through it, rather than exploiting it for our own ends. A triangular arrangement, rather than a linear one where God is at the top and the creation at the bottom, with humans in between. This is an arrangement of more equality. Changes in attitudes towards the creation have occurred during history, as described below.

Max-Neef (p. 6) writes that humankind, in relation to the whole of creation, has had choices between exploiting, or working with, the whole of creation. The path chosen on each occasion was one which treated nature as a commodity to be exploited. As Bacon said, the aim was to torture nature to get at her secrets. By the other path, that of St Francis, elements in nature were regarded as brothers and sisters. We can gain inspiration by making the connection between early Friends and the Spiritual Franciscans as described in chapter 3, however tenuous it may be. Quakers and the Spiritual Franciscans have in common the aim of a simple life style and a care for the rest of creation. These qualities are particularly needed at this time of crisis, but the human race, including Quakers, has taken a different path.

The change in Quakerism in the latter part of the 17th Century and subsequently has caused the experience of the new creation to be forced through a sieve, so that from the other side came a cluster of values: peace, simplicity, equality, justice, truth and integrity, while the spiritual source of these was filtered out.

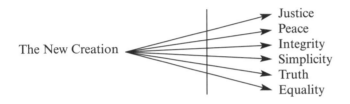

Ironically, the whole of creation was left behind in the sieving process and all the values are human-centered. The holistic and dynamic shift in vision of the New Creation was reduced to the somewhat mundane "testimonies" which have lost the inspiration of the founders. Lacking this vision it is difficult to engage modern Quakers with the realities of our situation and the testimonies are all anthropocentrically focussed. However, it is still possible for us to recapture some of this holistic experience, not necessarily dramatically as early Friends did, but gradually, as we learn more and more about the intricacies of relationships within nature, and we study both macro and micro parts of the universe. Slowly, as our consciousness changes, we become aware of the miracles around us and wonder more and more about our place.

Early Friends accepted the challenge of living as though the New Creation was manifest. Our challenge today is to live as members of the planetary community, making our contribution to the creation and respecting its other members.

10. NOTES

1. The word "creation" is mentioned many times by Fox and refers to "animals, plants, the sea, materials, weather…" (Pickvance, p. 64). Other Friends also used it, including Howgill, Burrough, Naylor, Farnsworth and Parnell. They held the whole of

creation to have a special sacred value, and the relationship of humans to it to be of fundamental importance.

2. An interesting digression is to compare the writings of Matthew Fox (1983) with those of Rufus Jones. Matthew Fox writes on "creation spirituality" which has a strong connection with the natural world, and which, he believes, has continued from the first conversions in Britain, although dominated by the orthodox, hierarchical type of Christianity. The people quoted by Fox (307-19) as belonging to the "creation spirituality" tradition are in many cases the same as those listed by Jones as being "spiritual reformers", for example, Ireneus, John the Scot, Hildegaard of Bingen, St Dominic, St Francis, Mechtild of Magdeburg, Eckhart, the Theologica Germanica, Sebastian Franck, and Hans Dencke. Fox also gives George Fox and John Woolman in his "Family Tree of Creation Spirituality". Concern about the whole of creation has increased greatly in the last few decades, and when Jones was writing it was largely ignored, which may account for his omission. I think that Rufus Jones and Matthew Fox would have enjoyed discussing these matters with one another.

3. Joachim is placed by Dante as XII in the outer circle of twelve lights in the Heaven of the Sun, Canto XII, where he is decribed as Calabria's abbot, "spirit-fired, and prophet true". The two circles represent the "divine union and inter-relation of love and learning". Most of those in the outer circle are followers of St Francis (Sayers and Reynolds p.161, 166-8).

4. Early Friends referred to animals as creatures, and as humans were also called creatures on occasion one has to know the context to distinguish between the meanings.

11. REFERENCES

Beatty, Edward Corbyn Obert (1975)
William Penn as Social Philosopher.
New York: Octagon Books.

Benson, Lewis (1976)
What did George Fox teach about Christ?
Gloucester: Fellowship Press, New Foundation.

Braithwaite, William C. (1921)
The Second Period of Quakerism. Introduction by Rufus Jones.
London: Macmillan and Co., Ltd.

Braithwaite, William C. (1961)
The Second Period of Quakerism, 2nd edn, prepared by
Henry J.Cadbury, Introduction by Frederick B. Tolles.
York: William Sessions Ltd.

Braithwaite, William C. (1981)
The Beginnings of Quakerism to 1660. 2nd edn.
Revised by Henry J. Cadbury.
York: William Sessions Ltd.

Brockbank Elizabeth (1949)
Edward Burrough, A Wrestler for Truth 1634 - 1662.
London: Bannisdale Press.

Burrough, Edward (1672)
Works.
York: T. Sowle.

Burrough, Edward (1658)
A Standard lifted up and an Ensign held forth to all Nations. Ch. XII.
London: Giles Calvert.

Callaway, Henry (1846)
A Memoir of James Parnell with extracts from his writings.
London: Charles Gilpin.

Clarke, George (1987)
John Bellers, 1674-1725, Quaker Visionary, His Life and Times, and Writing.
York: Sessions Book Trust.

Clarkson, Thomas (1807)
A Portraiture of Quakerism, Vol III. 2nd edn.,
London: Longman, Hurst, Rees and Orme.

Cragg, Gerald (1970)
The Church and the Age of Reason 1648-1789.
London: Penguin, reprinted with revisions.

Damrosch, Leo (1996)
The Sorrows of the Quaker Jesus and the Puritan Crackdown on the Free Spirit.
Cambridge, Mass: Harvard University Press.

Fox, George (1657) Concerning Good Morrow, and Good
Even: the World 's Customs but by the Light which into the World has come.
London: Thomas Simmons, Tracts 22.

Fox, George (1990) *Works* Vol 1. Reprinted from 1831.
Philadelphia: New Foundation Publication

Fox ,George. (1990) *Works* Vol. 2

Fox, George (1990) *Works* Vol. 7

Fox, George (1990) *Works* Vol. 8
Epistle 292 To Friends in New England, Virginia and Barbados 1672.

Fox, Matthew (1983)
Original Blessing: A Primer in Creation Spirituality Presented in Four Paths,
Twenty-Six themes and Two Questions.
Santa Fe, New Mexico: Bear & Company Ltd.

Freiday, Dean (1990)
Response to A Quaker Theology of the Stewardship of Creation by Virginia
Schurman in *Quaker Religious Thought* no. 24

Freiday, Dean (ed) (1967)
Barclay's *Apology in Modern English,* 3rd printing.
New Jersey: Monthly Meeting of Friends in Philadelphia. 392

Goodwin, J. in *Hagiomastix* 1646.
Preface. In Hill, Christopher. 1975.
The World Turned upside Down Harmondsworth,
Middlesex: Penguin Books.

Gwyn, Douglas (reprint 1991)
Apocalypse of the Word: The Life and Message of George Fox. Richmond,
IN: Friends United Press.

Gwyn, Douglas (1995)
The Covenant Crucified, Quakers and the Rise of Capitalism.
Wallingford, Pennsylvania: Pendle Hill Publications.

Gwyn, Douglas (1998)
The Covenant of Light in *Heaven on Earth, Quakers and the Second Coming*
by Ben Pink Dandelion, Douglas Gwyn and Timothy Peat.
Birmingham and Kelso: Woodbrooke College and Curlew Productions.

Hayes, Will (1942)
Grey Ridge, The Book of Francis Howgill. Meopham Green,
Kent: Order of the Great Companions.

Heer, Friedrich (1961)
The Medieval World, Europe 1100-1350, translated from the
German by Janet Sondheimer.
New York and Toronto: The New American Library.

Hill, Christopher (1975)
The World Turned Upside Down, Radical Ideas During the English Revolution.
Harmondsworth, Middlesex: Penguin Books.

Jones, Rufus. (1921, 2nd impression, 1st edn. 1919 in Introduction to
The Second Period of Quakerism by William C. Braithwaite.
London: MacMillan and Co.Ltd.

Jones, Rufus (1928, 1st edn. 1914)
Spiritual Reformers of the Sixteenth and Seventeenth Centuries.
London: MacMillan and Co. Ltd.

Jones, Rufus M. (1936, 1st edn.1909)
Studies in Mystical Religion.
London: MacMillan and Co. Ltd.

Jones, Rufus M. (1932)
Mysticism and Democracy in the English Commonwealth
Cambridge, Mass.: Harvard University Press

Jones, T. Canby (1989)
The Power of the Lord is Over All:The Pastoral Letters of George Fox.
Richmond, Indiana: Friends United Press.

Keiser, R.Melvin (1991)
The Inward Light and the New Creation.
Pendle Hill Pamphlet 295, Wallingford, PA .

Lawson, Thomas (1679)
Dagon's Fall before the Ark.
London: T. Sowle, reprint 1703.

Loukes, Harold (1997)
Friends Face reality trans. by Margaret Kohl.
London: The Bannisdale Press.

Max-Neef, Manfred (2008)
The Forgotten Map in *Resurgence* No. 247 March/April.

Morries Geoffrey Peter (2010) *From Revelation to Resource, The Natural World in the Thought and Experience of Quakers in Britain and Ireland, 1647-1830.* A Thesis submitted to the University of Birmingham for the Degree of Doctor of Philosophy.

Naylor, James (2007) Love to the Lost in
The Works of James Naylor (1618-1660)1656. Vol 3. Farmington,
ME: Quaker Heritage Press.

Nickalls, John L. (ed) (1975)
The Journal of George Fox.
London: Religious Society of Friends.

Nuttall, Geoffrey F. (1947)
"Unity with the Creation": George Fox and the Hermetic Philosophy.
Friends Quarterly, New Series No. 3 July 1947.

Nuttall, Geoffrey F. (1975) Introduction to
The Journal of George Fox, edited by John L. Nickalls,
London: Religious Society of Friends.

Parnell, James, (1675)
Collection of the Several Writings Given forth from the Spirit of the Lord through the Meek, Patient and Suffering Servant of God.

Penn, William (1825)
Select Works, Vol. 3, 4th edn.
London: William Phillips.

Penn, William (1961) in Braithwaite,
The Second Period of Quakerism

Pennington, Isaac (1996)
Works Vol. 3. Glenside,
PA: Quaker Heritage Press

Pickvance Joseph (1989)
A Reader's Companion to George Fox's Journal,
London: Quaker Home Service.

Regenstein, Lewis G. (1991) *Replenish the Earth:*
A History of Organised Religions Treatment of Animals and Nature - Including the Biblical Message of Conservation and Kindness to Animals. London: SCM Press.

Sayers, Dorothy L. and Barbara Reynolds, translated by (1962)
The Comedy of Dante Alighieri, the Florentine, Cantica III Paradise (Il Paradiso).
Harmondsworth, Middlesex: Penguin Books

Schurman, Virginia (1990).
A Quaker Theology of the Stewardship of Creation.
Quaker Religious Thought, Vol. 24.

Taylor, Thomas (1660)
A Testimony for the Lord God and his Works in the Earth.
Tracts, Ashworth: Vol. 2, Tract 5.

Taylor Thomas,(1697)
Truth's innocency and simplicity shining,
London: T. Sowle.

Thomas, Keith (1984)
Man and the Natural World, Changing attitudes in England, 1500-1800,
London: Penguin.

Tolles, Frederick B. (1961) introduction to
The Second Period of Quakerism 2nd edn. by William C. Braithwaite.
York: Sessions.

Wilcox Catherine (1995)
Theology and Women's Ministry in seventeenth century English Quakerism,
Lampeter: Edwin Mellen.

Wilson, Lloyd Lee (2001),
Essays on the Quaker Vision of Gospel Order.
Philadelphia, PA: Quaker Press of Friends General Conference.

Whittaker E. Jean, (1986)
Thomas Lawson, North Country Botanist, Quaker and Schoolmaster.
York: Sessions.